AMERICAN ANTIQUE GLASS

by
ELIZABETH OLIVER

illustrated by
REBECCA A. MERRILEES

GOLDEN PRESS · NEW YORK
Western Publishing Company, Inc.
Racine, Wisconsin

ACKNOWLEDGMENTS

In the preparation of *American Antique Glass*, I am indebted to many students of glass on whose research this book has been based. I am also indebted to the many museums that I have visited and to private collectors who have helped me with suggestions, information, and the loan of pieces from their collections.

Among these are the Bennington Museum, Bennington, Vt.; Chrysler Museum, Norfolk, Va., Corning Museum of Glass, Corning, N.Y.; Greenfield Village and Henry Ford Museum, Dearborn, Mich.; Old Sturbridge Village, Sturbridge, Mass.; Portland Museum of Art, Portland, Maine; Sandwich Glass Museum, Sandwich, Mass.; Toledo Museum of Art, Toledo, Ohio; and the Wadsworth Atheneum Museum, Hartford, Ct.

In particular, I express appreciation to Eugene R. Kosche, assistant curator, the Bennington Museum, who has been most generous not only in giving his time, but also in making available for illustrations many pieces from the Museum's glass collection.

Special thanks go to Charles B. Gardner, New London, Ct., who read and corrected the bottle section of the manuscript, to Mrs. H. Virginia Butterfield, Bolton Notch, Ct., who lent many pieces of glass from her collection for illustrations, and to J. Richard Gothold, Wethersfield, Ct., for the use of bottles from his pharmaceutical collection.

I express appreciation to my consultant, Dr. Milton Hopkins, Port Washington, Long Island, N.Y., who guided the development of the book and who was always on hand to advise, and to my editor, Mrs. Vera Webster, without whose countless hours and determination the book would never have been finished.

And most of all, I pay tribute to the memory of my dear mother, who participated in the project from its beginning, accompanying me on visits to museums, assisting with the research and encouraging me all along the way.

Elizabeth Oliver

CONTENTS

(1) Roman, Rhineland-patterned molded ewer, 3rd–4th century BC; (2) Egypt, 18th Dynasty cored amphoriskos; (3) Egypt, stone and glass beads, CA. 1800 BC; (4) Roman, probably Gaul bottle, 2nd–4th century; (5) Roman, cameo cup, 1st–2nd century; (6) Roman, Rhineland footed beaker, 3rd–4th century.

HISTORY OF GLASSMAKING

When did man first discover that he could turn the sands in the river beds and from the mountainsides into glass, one of the most versatile and remarkable products ever developed? When did man learn that, in much the same way as volcanic fires, over aeons of time, produced obsidian and other forms of natural glass from the silica beneath the earth's surface, he too could make glass?

No one knows a precise answer to these questions. It is believed, however, that sometime between 4000 and 3000 B.C. glass was being made along the shores of the Mediterranean—probably in Mesopotamia or Egypt, or both—and that glass in its earliest form was used as a glaze with which to cover stone beads. It is also believed that the first all-glass vessels were made in Egypt sometime between 1600 and 1500 B.C. These were made, not by blowing or pressing, but by lining a core with molten glass and then removing the core.

The development of the blowpipe, probably by the Syrians or Egyptians around 100 B.C., was a revolutionary step in the history of glassmaking. Some researchers equate its importance with Owens' invention of the automatic blowing machine (p. 125) in the United States in 1891. With the advent of the blowpipe, glass could be blown relatively quickly and easily into useful shapes and forms.

When the Romans conquered Egypt, they took the blowpipe with them; and, during the next five hundred years, they developed the art of glassblowing to a level some people believe has never been surpassed. Many of the decorative techniques used today—cameo cutting, casing, and applied glass, such as prunts, threads, and looping—were created or refined by the Romans.

Glass blowing in ancient Egypt; line engraving after a relief.

THE DECLINE of the glassblowing industry in western Europe began with the collapse of the Roman civilization. Only in the East did the skill continue to develop. The Syrians were distinguished particularly for their gilding and enameling techniques. It was not until about 1250 A.D. that the art of glassmaking was revived in western Europe. Venice was its new center, and by 1500 the Venetians were making some of the finest glass the world has ever seen. Among the many techniques they developed that were later used by American glassmakers were latticinio (2), millefiori (3), and engraving (5).

Over the next three or four hundred years, Venetian skills gradually spread to the lowland countries, France, and England. About the same time the Germans, less influenced by the Venetians, were developing their own distinctive style and techniques (4).

The development of a new formula for lead glass in England by George Ravenscroft in 1675 marked the end of Italy's influence and the emergence of England as the new leader. Ravenscroft's formula made possible a heavy brilliant glass (1), usually decorated with deep cutting, quite unlike the thin, fragile Venetian glass. English and Irish glass became the dominant influence on early American fine glass.

EARLY AMERICAN GLASS is of two types—soda-lime and lead. Sand is the basic ingredient in both. Soda-lime glass (1–6) was used for making window panes, bottles and household utensils designed for everyday use. The same formula is still used for making some ninety percent of the glass produced today. Soda-lime glass in its natural colors—greens, olive ambers, and ambers—derived from metallic substances in the sand is known as "bottle glass" or "green glass." It was used chiefly by the early glassmakers for bottles and window glass.

Lead glass (7–9), costly then as now, was used only for finer wares. Its softness lends itself to cutting. Lead also gives the glass a brilliance, which is enhanced by deep cuttings that increase the refraction of light.

COLORED GLASS was popular in the early days. As a matter of fact, artificially colored glass was produced even before clear glass. The color in most of the earliest American glass (1–3) was not artificially produced, however, but resulted from impurities, such as iron, in the sand. Finer glassware was made colorless by the addition of manganese to the metal. Care had to be taken not to add too much manganese to the metal, or the glass would become purple after it had been exposed to bright sunlight over a period of time.

Various oxides were used to create different colors of glass. Blue was created by the addition of cobalt (6); green by adding copper and iron (7); ruby by adding copper and gold (4); amethyst (5) and purple by adding black oxide. In addition to the various oxides, various temperatures would change the same formula into different colors. For example, certain greens, when overheated, would change to amethyst (5).

THREE METHODS of making glass were used by early American glassmakers: it was blown, molded, or pressed. Blown glass (pp. 10–11) was entirely free blown. Molded glass (p. 12) was formed by blowing the mass (parison) of molten glass into a mold. Pressed glass (p. 13) was made by pouring the hot liquid into a press, operated by hand.

BLOWN GLASS represents the highest level of glassmaking, both in artistry and skill. It was the first method used in making glass in America, and the techniques used today vary little from those of the past. At least three people are required —the gaffer, or master blower; a gatherer, or servitor; and a helper. Together they form a shop, or chair. The basic tools are the blowpipe, a metal tube from 2½ to 6 feet long (1); a pontil rod on which the object is held while it is being shaped (2); the pucellas used in shaping the object (3); wood jack (4), battledore (5); shears (6); cut-off shears (7); and block (8).

1

2

3

4

5

6

7

8

9

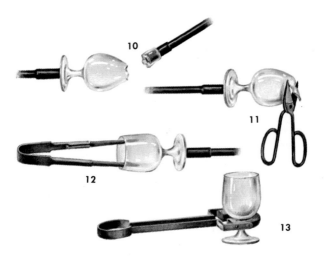

STEPS IN BLOWING A GOBLET

1. A gather of molten glass (metal) is taken from furnace on heated blowpipe.

2. Gather is rolled on marver to center and chill it.

3. Gather is inflated slightly to form bubble. This is called a "parison." A second gather is taken over the first and again inflated slightly.

4. Parison is shaped in block.

5. Necking the parison: a groove is made by applying pressure with pucellas just beyond the blowpipe. This will later be used as break-off point of goblet.

6. End of parison is flattened on paddle called a battledore.

7. Third gather is taken for stem on heated pontil rod, attached to the base, sheared off and then shaped with pucellas.

8. Fourth gather is taken on heated pontil rod, added to stem and a foot is formed between leaves of clapper.

9. Pontil rod attached to foot.

10. Blowpipe is knocked off.

11. Rim is heated in "glory hole" and trimmed with shears.

12. Goblet is heated again and shaped with wood jack.

13. Pontil rod is knocked off and goblet is taken by carrying fork to annealing oven.

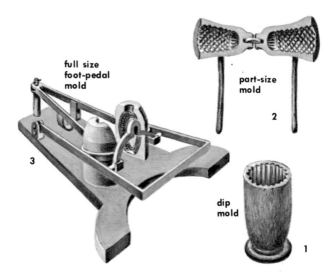

full size
foot-pedal
mold

part-size
mold

2

3

dip
mold

1

MOLDED GLASS is glass made by blowing the molten metal into a mold; the object derives part or all of its shape and often its pattern from the mold. Early American glass was blown in both dip molds (1) and piece molds (2, 3)—part-size and full-size. Molds occurred either with or without a design impressed intaglio on the inside. Glass blown in a part-size mold with an intaglio design is called pattern-molded glass. Decoration created in this manner is known as pattern-molding. Pattern molding was a frequent form of decoration of early American glassmakers. The parison was blown into the part-size mold, then it was removed and the glassmaker expanded it by blowing it again. The larger he blew it, the less distinct became the pattern. Commonly used patterns included vertical ribbing (4), fluting (5), diamond (6), diamond daisy (10), and checkered diamond (9). Diagonal or swirled ribbing (7) was achieved by placing the parison in the mold in a diagonal position and twirling it slightly. Broken swirl ribbing (8) was created by reheating the gather after it had been removed from the mold and placing it in the mold again and twisting it.

A variation of molded glass—formed by blowing hot metal into a full-size mold consisting usually of three hinged pieces—is referred to by most collectors as Blown Three-Mold (p. 24).

PRESSED GLASS is glass made by pressing hot metal in a mold in which it has been poured. Unitl 1827 it was made in a small hand-operated mold (11). The development of a new type of pressing machine marked an important American contribution to glassmaking by making possible the production of glass on a larger scale and thus paving the way for mass production. The glass was made by gathering a glob of hot metal on the pontil rod and pouring it into the mold. A plunger operated by a lever was then brought down, forcing the liquid into all parts of the mold. The moldmaker, not the glassmaker, determined the design and, in part, the quality.

GLASSMAKERS

The first glasshouse to be established in America was in Jamestown, Virginia, in 1608. Nothing is known about it except that it was no longer in operation by 1617.

Between 1621 and 1622, a second glasshouse was founded. Its main function was to manufacture beads for use as currency in the fur trade with the Indians. Many beads have been found in Indian graves in Pennsylvania and Florida, but no evidence has been found that they were made in Jamestown.

CASPAR WISTAR established about 1739, in Salem County, New Jersey, the first glasshouse to operate successfully over a period of years in America. Like most of the early eighteenth century American glassmakers, Wistar was from Germany. His main products were window glass and bottles, but he also made bowls, jars for jam, and other household items. Because his wares were unmarked, and resembled in form, technique and decoration those of other South Jersey glassmakers, it is almost impossible to attribute positively any pieces of glass to Wistar. The type of glass he made, however, is known through advertisements and shards found near the factory site.

sugar bowl

SOUTH JERSEY GLASS is identifiable with folk art by the manner in which it was fashioned and its general features. Each piece was blown and decorated, usually by manipulation rather than pattern molded (7) according to the will of the glassblower. It was made mostly from bottle glass in natural colors.

DECORATION on South Jersey glass usually is applied glass. It is done by applying glass in its molten state to the object while the glass is still hot. The lily pad (1, 4) is the most distinctive applied glass decoration on South Jersey glass. It also appears on glass made later in New York (4) and New Hampshire. Other applied glass decorations on South Jersey glass include prunts (2), quilling (8), threading (1, 4), gadrooning (3), and looping (5, 6), rigaree (9). Looping is done by applying loops of a different color of molten glass on the object and then pressing it onto the surface so that it appears to be imprinted. Red, white, and blue were the main colors used in looping on South Jersey glass.

HENRY STIEGEL, another German settler, established in Pennsylvania the second important glass house in America. He was the first glassmaker known to have produced table and decorative wares commercially. The variety and quality of his products and the extent of his output put him in the forefront of America's early glassmakers. A colorful figure who indulged his taste for extravagant and grandiose living, he was known as the "Baron."

Stiegel established the first of his three glasshouses at Elizabeth Furnace, west of what is now Reading, in 1763. In 1764, he began construction of a glasshouse in Manheim, and three years later undertook his most ambitious project, a larger house, also in Manheim, where some of his finest glass was produced. Overextension in a period of political and economic stress, following the passage of the Stamp Act, created financial difficulties, which culminated in the utter failure of his business in 1774. Stiegel himself was imprisoned briefly for debt.

Stiegel designed his wares to compete with fine glassware imported from England and the continent. Unlike South Jersey glass, where design was highly individualistic and generally inspired by the fancy of the glassmaker, Stiegel's followed the European tradition. His wares included decanters, flips, mugs, wine glasses, water tumblers, sugar bowls, salts, cruets, bottles and other forms, which were sold widely in Boston, New York, Baltimore and Pennsylvania. He made both lead and soda-lime glass, clear and colored—particularly blue, amethyst and purple.

Because Stiegel's wares resembled European pieces so closely in form, technique and design, few, if any, pieces can be positively attributed to him. Consequently, glass resembling that he is known to have made is referred to as Stiegel-type.

ENAMELED PEASANT MOTIFS on Stiegel-type glass are a characteristic European form of decoration. Hearts, birds, and flowers are among the motifs that appear on small bottles (1, 2), glasses (3), and other pieces. He favored certain colors of enamels; he was particularly fond of deep blue.

COPPER-WHEEL ENGRAVING (4, 6, 7) also occurs on Stiegel-type pieces. Frequently, the engraving is a band of tiny leaves or flowers. Engravings appear only on the clear, or uncolored pieces, however.

PATTERN MOLDING is another decorative technique on Stiegel-type glass. Patterns include the diamond (9, 10), diamond daisy (11), and daisy-in-hexagon (5). Most pattern-molded pieces occur in colors (8, 9, 10, 11).

JOHN FREDERICK AMELUNG was the first glassmaker in America to produce glass that was comparable to quality European glass. It was the finest glass produced in America in the 18th century. Amelung was the first glassmaker in America to sign some of his pieces. He founded his glasshouse after the American Revolutionary War in Frederick County, Maryland in 1785. He called the place New Bremen after his native Bremen in Germany. Amelung's wares include decanters, goblets, tumblers and other drinking vessels, and pokals (1). Pokals are covered glass goblets or chalices.

COPPER-WHEEL ENGRAVING on Amelung glass is distinguished for both the artistry of the design and the craftsmanship (1–4). The delicate wreath or medallion of tiny leaves or flowers or both is almost an Amelung trademark. Many of Amelung's finest pieces were designed for gifts and frequently the name or initials of the person for whom the piece was made are inscribed in beautiful script inside the medallion. Among his best known pieces are the Schley and Bremen pokals. The latter was presented to his financial supporters in Bremen, Germany, in 1788. He also used gilding and enameling as decoration.

PATTERN MOLDING is another form of decoration believed to have been used by Amelung. Fragments of bottles of checkered-diamond design have been found near the Amelung Glass works, substantiating the possibility that the flask to the left (5) is an Amelung piece.

THE PITKIN FAMILY founded a glasshouse in East Manchester, Connecticut in 1783. It continued to operate until about 1830. Few pieces can be positively identified as Pitkin, but pieces found in the area indicate that the house probably made pitchers, bowls, inkwells (1), bottles (2, 3, 4) and other household utensils (5). Indeed, the house is known today for the so-called Pitkin bottles made there.

ALBERT GALLATIN, a native Swiss, who later became a United States Senator and Secretary of the Treasury, was interested in developing American industries. Gallatin was responsible for establishing the first glassworks in the midwestern area. The midwestern area, as the section west of Pittsburgh is known to glass collectors, was the site for the first glassworks in New Geneva, Pennsylvania, on the Monongahela River, in 1797. Some twenty years later, Gallatin's associates, Baltzer and his family, built another glasshouse across the river in Greensboro. The two glasshouses are known to have made pitchers, sugar bowls, milk bowls (6), goblets (7) and other household glassware. The only molds known to be in existence today in which glass was pattern molded are those used in these two glasshouses.

BAKEWELL AND COMPANY of Pittsburgh and the New England Glass Company of East Cambridge were the two major glass houses established in the first two decades of the 19th century. War, depression, and the flooding of the market by English exporters all contributed to the high casualty rate of the many glass houses founded prior to 1820.

Bakewell and Company, founded in 1808, is attributed with having been the first successful flint-glass house in the United States and the first to make cut glass (1), commercially. It made all types of plain, molded, cut and engraved, and pressed ware.

THE NEW ENGLAND GLASS COMPANY, founded in 1817 by Deming Jarves, ranks as one of the largest and finest producers of glass in the 19th century and has the longest unbroken record in the manufacture of glass. "Every description of glassware, from a simple pressed wine glass to the most elaborately cut and richly plated, silvered, and engraved glassware is produced here in a style of beauty and excellence (2, 3, 4) unrivaled in the world . . ." wrote *Gleason's Pictorial* in its November 8, 1851, issue. In 1888, the company, which had been bought by W. L. Libbey and later became the Libbey Glass Company, was moved to Toledo, Ohio, where it continued to make fine cut glass.

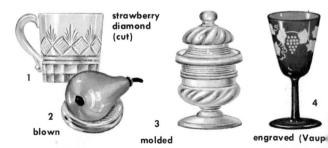

1
strawberry diamond (cut)

2
blown

3
molded

4
engraved (Vaup

threading (Lutz)

lacy glass

acanthus leaf

Sandwich Star pattern glass

salt

dolphin candle-stick

tieback

ruby overlay fingerbowl

THE BOSTON AND SANDWICH COMPANY, established in 1825 on Cape Cod by Deming Jarves after disassociating himself from the New England Glass Company, also made all kinds of glassware—blown, molded, and pressed. It is known especially, however, for its lacy glass. The name ''Sandwich'' has become almost synonymous with ''lacy glass.'' The style and quality of much of its glass are very similar to that of the New England Glass Co. and often cannot be distinguished.

THE MT. WASHINGTON GLASS WORKS was still another glasshouse founded in South Boston, Massachusetts by Deming Jarves in 1837. This house, which made fine blown and cut glass, moved to New Bedford in 1869. It later became part of the Pairpoint Manufacturing Company, known for its art glass (p. 78).

NEW HAMPSHIRE AND VERMONT were the sites of some dozen 19th-century bottle and window glass houses. The Keene (Marlboro Street) Glass Works, established in 1815, is known for its fine figured flasks, particularly the Masonic (1, 1a), made of flint glass in green, blue, amethyst, purple and clear, and the sunburst (4); decanters; inkwells (3); and other household articles. Four Stoddard (New Hampshire) glasshouses produced Ludlows, flasks (7, 7a), other bottles, and some pitchers, predominantly amber (2). Four Vermont houses, established between 1812 and 1832, made free-blown pitchers, bowls, drugstore bottles (6), chemistry bottles (5), and other pieces from window glass.

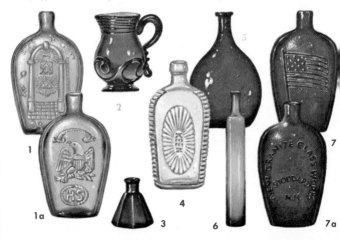

NEW JERSEY AND NEW YORK also had numerous bottle and window-glass houses in the 19th century, which made jars, pitchers, bowls, vases and candlesticks. Blown glass produced in New York houses (1, 2) tended to follow the south Jersey tradition, especially in the use of the lilypad (1), which they generally improved.

THE MIDWEST, especially Zanesville, Mantua, and Kent, Ohio produced flasks, bottles, and other household wares that are outstanding both in color and design (3, 4, 5, 6, 7, 8). Pattern molding was the characteristic form of decoration—particularly 16-, 20-, 24-, and 32-rib molds; 10- and 15-diamond molds. Ravenna was the site of what was probably a major bottle (4) manufacturer.

GLASS TYPES

In the early 1800's American glassmakers were faced with the need to find a way to manufacture glass in larger quantities and in unique varieties. The Irish and English imports that had been flooding the market were gone, and high tariffs were forcing the growth of American industry. The fast-growing population of the young republic needed all kinds of glassware.

BLOWN THREE-MOLD GLASS

About 1820, a variation in blown glass was developed by American glassmakers that could be produced in larger quantities and thus more cheaply. This type of glass is referred to by most people as Blown Three-Mold. It gets its name from the full-size, usually three-part mold (p. 25), into which the gather of glass was blown. The parts or pieces of the mold were joined together by hinges. Some molds consisted of two, four, or even five pieces, but the glass is still known as Blown Three-Mold. Seam marks where the mold was joined provide one means of identifying this type.

Often two or more forms were blown in the same mold. Pitchers, for instance, were blown in molds made for decanters, lamps and candlesticks in molds for stoppers. Bowls and celery vases were blown mostly in decanter and flip molds; hats in molds made for inkwells and castor bottles.

Blown Three-Mold glass was made in almost every form for the table and for general use. Most pieces are of fine flint glass that is heavy and brilliant and has a clear ring when struck. Most flint pieces are clear, although some occur in sapphire blue, purple blue, and

Sectioned molds were used to impress
designs on blown glass.

gray blue. Some Blown Three-Mold was also made of
window and bottle glass. These pieces occur in olive
amber, olive green, and aquamarine.

THE DESIGNS on Blown Three-Mold glass come from the
mold. The design on the outside is exactly opposite to
that on the inside of the object. Lines that are convex
on the outside are concave on the inside and vice versa.

About 150 designs are known to have been made in
Blown Three-Mold glass. Collectors of American antique
glass classify these designs into three general groups:
Geometric (1), Arch (2), and Baroque (3).

Geometric
(vertical
ribbing with
diamond diapering)

Arch (Gothic
arch above
ribs)

Baroque
(shell and
ribbing)

1

2

3

GEOMETRIC DESIGNS were the earliest and the most numerous of the three groups. These were largely imitations of cut glass patterns for which Blown Three-Mold glass sought to be a substitute. Designs include ribbings (1, a, b, c), flutings (2, 3), circles (5) and ovals, diamond diapering and diamonds (3, 6, 7, 8). All occur in many variations and combinations. Most patterns contain at least two different geometric designs. Ribbing—vertical (1), horizontal (1a), spiral (1b), or diagonal (1c)—occurs in some form in almost all geometric patterns (4). Diamond diapering often appears in combination with vertical ribbing.

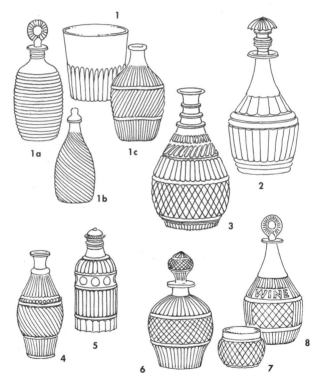

THE SUNBURST (1–11) is one of the most common motifs. It appears in many variations: Sunburst-in-Square (1, 2), Bull's Eye Sunburst (7), Diamond Sunburst (9), Waffle Diamond Sunburst (10), and Waffle Sunburst (11). Sunburst motifs are particularly popular today. Numbers 12–14 are diamond motifs.

Designs adapted from McKearin

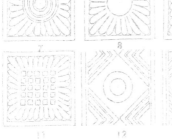

Some typical base designs

GLASS OBJECTS blown in geometric designs include every Blown Three Mold form—pitchers, decanters, goblets, sugar bowls, celery vases, toilet bottles, inkwells, salts, lamps, candlesticks, flip glasses, hats and witchballs. Pitchers were blown in at least thirty different geometric patterns. They are mostly quart and pint sizes, without a foot. One of the most common patterns in which pitchers were blown has a wide band of diamond diapering between bands of vertical ribbing.

Decanters, though scarce like all Blown Three-Mold objects, are the most available in the geometric pattern. Stoppers for decanters and other bottles were made in Blown Three-Molds, as well as pressed and pattern-molded.

29

THE ARCH PATTERNS (1, 5) were made in far fewer forms and quantity than the Geometric. Articles were mostly decanters, pitchers and tumblers. The principal motif is an arch, Gothic (1) or Roman (5). Only eight Arch patterns are known, the most common of which is the Boston and Sandwich Arch and Fern Leaf with a medallion formed by two snakes (1). Decanters, both quart and pint sizes, were made in this particular pattern. Some decanters have inscribed in the medallion the name of a liquor—CHERRY, WHISKEY, WINE, BRANDY, RUM, or GIN. On one decanter GIN is upside down and reversed—NIϽ.

THE BAROQUE PATTERNS (2, 3, 4, 6) occur far more widely than the Arch, but less commonly than the Geometric. As in the Arch patterns, most articles are decanters, pitchers and tumblers. Baroque designs are the most elaborate of the Blown Three Mold groups. Like the Arch, the designs are in high relief. The principal motifs include ribs, shells, stars, trefoils and guilloches. The Horn of Plenty (2), Heart with Chain (4), Horizontal Palm Leaf, p. 31 (1), and Shell and Ribbing, p. 25 (3) are among the most common designs. Most forms are of clear glass, but creamers in the Trefoil and Ribbed (3) and Horizontal Palm Leaf patterns occur in grayish purple or blue as well as in clear glass. Creamers in Shell and Ribbing, p. 31 (3) were made in purple and decanters in blue.

IDENTIFYING THE ORIGIN of a piece of Blown Three-Mold glass may be difficult. Because different factories often used the same mold, it is impossible in many instances to attribute a particular piece to a specific factory. The Boston and Sandwich Glass Company was one of the earliest houses to make Blown Three-Mold glass. It was also made in South Cambridge, Massachusetts; Keene, New Hampshire; Coventry, Connecticut; Vernon, New York; and Kent, Ohio. It was more widely made in the East than in the Midwest. Glass made in some factories and areas do have identifiable characteristics—patterns, shapes, and even colors, such as the predominant bottle glass green and amber in New Hampshire.

SANDWICH glass is found in more than two dozen patterns in Geometric (2, 4), Arch, and Baroque (1—Horizontal Palm Leaf and 3-Shell and Ribbing). The base frequently has concentric rings or rays.

MIDWESTERN glass occurs in several Geometric patterns attributed to Ohio (5, 6). A Baroque pattern is attributed to Pittsburgh (7). Sugar bowls tend to be higher in proportion to diameter than Eastern.

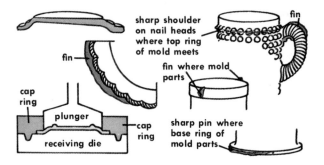

sharp shoulder on nail heads where top ring of mold meets

fin

fin

fin where mold parts

cap ring

plunger

cap ring

receiving die

sharp pin where base ring of mold parts

PRESSED GLASS

Pressed glass, which includes both lacy and pattern, offers the collector the widest variety of early American glass. Its development was motivated by the need for glassmakers to supply the growing demand for inexpensive tableware. Production increased as a result of a new pressing machine developed largely by Deming Jarves of the Boston and Sandwich Company in the late 1820's.

Pressed glass derives its design from the mold into which the molten glass is dropped. Unlike blown-molded glass, the edges of its patterns and its rims are sharp. The inside, or the side on which the pattern has not been pressed, is smooth.

The quality of a piece of pressed glass depends not only upon the condition of the mold in which it is pressed, but also upon the skill of the operator. The parts of the mold had to be perfectly adjusted and the precise amount of metal needed for the piece dropped into the mold. If there was too little, the pattern would be incomplete. If too much, the article would be too thick, with "fins" often formed at the seams, between the parts of the mold or on the edges or rim. The plunger, when rammed down into the mold, had to be in an exactly vertical line, with equal pressure exerted uniformly on the molten metal, or the piece would be of unequal thickness.

Imperfections such as these occur on the earliest forms of tableware, which are heavy and usually crude; but, with the exception of fins such imperfections disappeared as the operators gained more skill. The cap ring (see below), developed in 1829, was used to control the thickness of the rim on plates. It was attached to the mold and often provided the pattern of the shoulder as well as of the rim.

The earliest forms of pressed glass were knobs for doors and furniture (5) curtain tiebacks, salts (6), and cup plates. Designs were usually geometrical, inspired by the prestigious cut glass. Ribbing (1) and the waffle (4) motifs occur on early plates. The fan (4) was a popular border motif. The heart (2) also appears in many early designs, as well as the shield and pine tree (3).

LACY GLASS

By 1830, new designs, not influenced by cut glass designs, had begun to evolve. A new decorating technique called stippling was originated. Designed to compensate for the cold molds, which robbed the glass metal of its brilliance, the tiny dots added a refractory quality that lent a silvery sheen to the glass.

Lacy glass, as glass with a stippled background came to be called, was produced widely between the late 1830's and the early 1840's. The largest producer was the Sandwich Glass Company. Other houses, known to have made stippled ware, though in smaller quantities, were the New England Glass Company, the Union Glass Works and Fort Pitts Glass Works in Pittsburgh, Ritchie and Wheat of Wheeling, West Virginia, and glasshouses in the Philadelphia area.

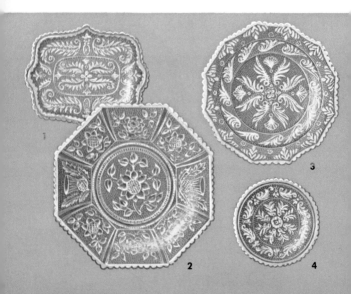